Kee Heung

家餅香奇

梅林園

Echoes of Old China

Echoes of Old China

TRADITIONAL SHOPS IN CONTEMPORARY HONG KONG

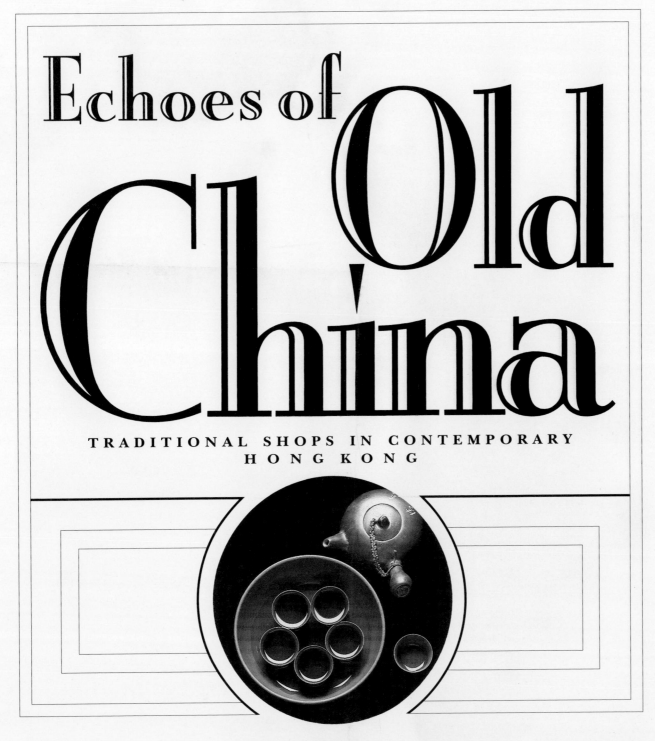

PHOTOGRAPHED BY BENNO GROSS & KWAN KWONG CHUNG, WRITTEN BY TREA WILTSHIRE

ECHOES OF OLD CHINA

Published by FormAsia Books Limited

2301 Sunning Plaza

10 Hysan Avenue, Hong Kong

Written by Trea Wiltshire

Edited by Zenobia Barlow

Photographed by Benno Gross and Kwan Kwong Chung

Designed by Lilian Tang Design Limited

Label Designs, courtesy of Joel Chung

© Text copyright, FormAsia Books Limited

© Photographs copyright, FormAsia Books Limited

First edition 1990/Second edition 1991

Printed by Paramount Printing Co. Limited

Printed in Hong Kong.

ISBN No. 962-7283-06-1

CONTENTS

Echoes of Old China *9*

Links with an almost Fabled Past *10*

And the catalyst was China Tea *12*

A philosophy of Cosmic Balance *26*

A Man's Fortune *40*

The Promise of Joy *50*

The Stone of Immortality *56*

Reverence for the Written Word *62*

The Ubiquitous Staple *70*

The Symbol of Light *84*

A Priceless Heritage *90*

Hong Kong has always had an insatiable appetite for the new and innovative — so no one is gambling on the future of a handful of traditional Chinese shops that are links with an almost fabled past. In these shops there is still time to relish the brushstrokes of fine calligraphy, to exchange niceties over a cup of fragrant tea, and to savour a lingering sense of formality and unhurried gentility......

Echoes of Old China

To me, Hong Kong's few remaining traditional shops are much more than mere shops. They are the last tangible links with a past that is fast being eclipsed by the cosmopolitan and contemporary.

The incense and paper shops nurture a blend of beliefs that, for thousands of years, has comforted those who worship at temples or shrines. The teashop evokes the romance of the early days of the China trade. The seal engraver, in his small street-side stall, symbolizes the artistry Chinese craftsmen have always employed to turn utilitarian objects into things of beauty.

When I returned to Hong Kong late last year to rediscover its traditional shops — shops that had caught the eye of two local photographers going about their business of portraying contemporary Hong Kong — I found the city much changed. And there was obsessive talk of greater changes. Of 1997.

Then on a peerless autumn afternoon, a friend took me to an old, almost deserted village in the New Territories.

The dragon hills were bathed in the mellow gold of the season and beyond them lay China. Hills circled the village itself, home now to only a few garrulous old Hakka women in black. One chatted to young relatives visiting from their high-rise apartment in Shatin — which the old woman would have known as a peaceful valley that once produced some of China's finest rice. A second woman slowly sifted the rice for the evening meal. A third noisily alerted us to the danger of a collapsed roof — its rafters broken, its tiles scattered. There were no men left to repair the roof, she complained. So the house lay open to tropical storms and the slow embrace of encroaching vegetation.

Walking away from the village we saw a line of low white-washed houses on a ridge beyond a tangled swathe of overgrown paddies. From a distance the string of houses looked completely deserted and appeared to have no road leading to it.

We started first on one path that dwindled and disappeared, then another that led to an impassable thicket. Finally we struck out across head-high undergrowth, sweating and dishevelled, but determined to reach the small collection of gabled houses.

Suddenly they were there before us — so silent, so obviously abandoned that we hesitated to disturb their dreaming. They stood slightly elevated above fields that must once have been burnished at this time of the year. There would have been a slow-moving buffalo, women patiently transplanting seedlings, children's voices in the groves of bamboo and coils of incense rising from a now forgotten shrine. The echoes of another era clung to the discoloured walls as surely as the patina of moss and miniature ferns that was slowly covering the roof tiles.

Within the encircling green hills I felt — as I had in some of the traditional shops — that there was nothing to indicate what century we were in. We had slipped back to an era as remote from the city we would return to as Imperial China is to the China of today.

The afternoon waned. Shadows enfolded the houses that were now boarded up, shuttered once again. Blind to the paddies that stretched before them. Deaf to the music of a nearby tumbling stream.

We cooled our faces in the stream's clear water and prepared to return to the city that now throbbed and glittered beyond the dark undulation of hills.

The question we carried away from the forgotten village remained unspoken: in the hyperactive Hong Kong of the 1990s, what will survive of Old China?

Trea Wiltshire, Hong Kong 1990

Links with an almost Fabled Past

mong Hong Kong's sheer towers and angular ultra-modern façades, a handful of traditional shops still survive in the city-port of the 1990s.

They lure the eye from deep-shaded porticoes dwarfed by high-rise apartments. They beckon from the faded, graceful terraces of a long-gone era.

In the context of Hong Kong which has always survived by selling — and today fills its expansive shop windows with every imaginable indulgence — they number but a few, and their merchandise is essentially modest.

You will find them in the older parts of the city where incense and the spice of street-side kitchens mingle in the shadow of tenements flagged with laundry. Or on outlying islands that dream in the South China Sea.

They are generally small shops, selling their wares in much the same way as in earlier generations. Their trading names and merchandise are carved on wooden boards in bold calligraphy, faded perhaps to mellow gold on red.

Once they may have been one of a street of shops selling similar wares — so that people spoke of jade street or bird street or lantern street when referring to them. Though a few such streets linger in Hong Kong, most of the shops are isolated not only by their own traditions, but by the physical demands of a land-hungry city that is forever re-emerging from its own destruction. Today, neighbouring shops purvey everything from laser printers to designer jeans.

As you enter beneath the carved calligraphy you are drawn back into another era by huge gilt-framed mirrors discoloured with age, and sepia portraits of a grandfather who left China to seek prosperity in the fast-growing colony. There may be polished wood, touches of brass, an occasional blackwood chair, framed testimonials from satisfied customers (each one a story worth hearing) or an appropriate couplet of high moral tone expressed in the finest calligraphy.

For in these shops there is still time to relish a brush stroke, to exchange niceties over a cup of fragrant tea, to savour the lingering sense of formality and unhurried gentility that is a world away from the brash salesmanship of city-hardened retailers.

The stories of the shops themselves soon become familiar. Most originated with a grandfather who fled the turmoil of China's famines, warlords or civil wars. He came with little, but put to work the skills acquired from his own father. He started with, perhaps, a small stall in Ladder Street, but when his son took over they moved to a better location — not so many steps for the old man who is now buried in China. The owner's father is now getting old, but he won't go back to China to die. Hong Kong is his home. Yes, business is good, but there is no need for a bigger shop. Who would run it? His children are studying computer science and engineering at the university......

The shop in which he sits could have been in the China of long ago. The skills he applies to his work echo those of craftsmen from the earliest days of the Chinese empire.

His shop is close-woven into the fabric of Chinese life, for there always were lanterns to light the festivals; paper shops to ease the passage of departing spirits; joss sticks to burn at temple shrines; or lucky finger jade to caress in the palm of one's hand.

There is thus a timeless quality about these shops. They sell things that the Chinese have always valued, be they things of beauty, or basics like rice or tea.

All are things that have been traded in Hong Kong since the birth of the colony in the 19th century, when a forgotten island of fisherfolk and temples became a base for foreign trade on the doorstep of China.

As such they are some of the last traces of Old China in the Hong Kong of today.

AND THE CATALYST WAS CHINA TEA

In the last century it was trade that first wove a tenuous thread between two remote empires, Britain and China.

The one sought trading outposts that would increase its mercantile might and advance its empire. The other — preserved in the amber of its own antiquity — seemed impervious to the challenge and change of a dawning era.

Britain was eager to lift the veil that Baron Macaulay claimed kept the world ignorant of the fabled empire that was the source of teas and silks, porcelain and lacquerware. China, long inured to dealing with other nations as vassal states paying tribute to the Middle Kingdom, saw trade as an intrusion. So it ignored the aggressive overtures of the distant island empire.

"Let China sleep…" warned Napoleon, but the "nation of shopkeepers" could not, for while the Imperial Dragon slept, it ignored the currents of trade, technology and revolution that swept beyond its borders.

When Britain went to war to defend its right to trade in China, the island of Hong Kong — along with other concessions — became the price of peace for China.

Soon a web of trade was being woven between the two empires from the colonial island moored off the southern sweep of the China coast.

Warehouses and colonnaded buildings multiplied along the waterfront. Clipper ships billowed in and out of the harbour carrying the handcrafted merchandise of China, and the industrial products of a world that would soon dispense with sail in favour of steam.

On the island's green flanks church spires and Victorian mansions vied with ancestral halls and porcelain-tiled temples. And in the city shops, ornamental fans and

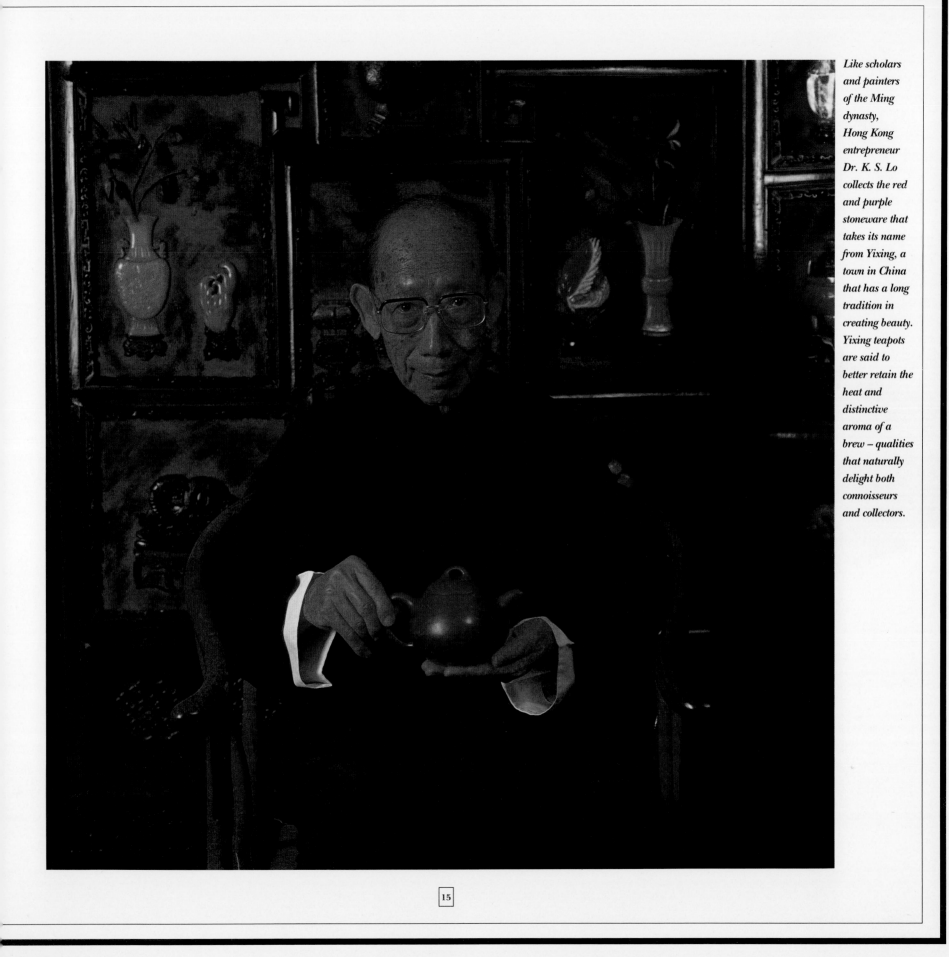

Like scholars and painters of the Ming dynasty, Hong Kong entrepreneur Dr. K. S. Lo collects the red and purple stoneware that takes its name from Yixing, a town in China that has a long tradition in creating beauty. Yixing teapots are said to better retain the heat and distinctive aroma of a brew – qualities that naturally delight both connoisseurs and collectors.

Since the 7th century, the Chinese have dried and smoked the leaf from its mountain tea gardens, savouring the infusion it created. Today in Hong Kong, the time-honoured ritual of taking tea begins with a visit to a traditional teashop, its pewter canisters and loft packed with a variety of fragrant brews from China.

Chinese silks shimmered beside machine-made brocades and the latest spring bonnets from Europe.

As Victorian globetrotters soon reported, an eastern entrepôt of untold potential was being created.

And the catalyst was China tea.

An Infusion of Tea Legend suggested that the very first brew of China tea was accidental. A fortuitous breeze is said to have plucked the leaves of wild tea trees and deposited them in a bowl of boiling water being prepared for an emperor of 5,000 years ago. Tempted by the aroma, the emperor sampled the infusion and pronounced himself well pleased with its soothing, yet reviving qualities. A tradition — and an industry — were thus born.

By the 7th century the custom of drying and smoking the leaves of the evergreen *Camellia sinensis* had become well established. Tea gardens flourished in many provinces and already the emperor received an annual tribute of tea from his subjects — a custom that survived to the last imperial dynasty.

However, ten centuries elapsed before the brew the Chinese called *t'e* or *ch'a* became fashionable in Europe.

Initially sold in Britain as a luxury cure-all for problems as diverse as "gripping of the guts" and dropsy, China tea soon became indispensable to the English way of life. Taken in the late afternoon it was said to dispel what the Duke of Bedford's wife described as "that sinking feeling".

Tea connoisseurs were soon rhapsodizing over the subtle variations of teas grown in different regions, for both soil and climate imparted different flavours. With countless varieties available, tea tasters sometimes blended up to 40 different teas to create the taste to temple a fickle market. And when the market insisted on "new season" teas, the

In Hong Kong no one gathers "heavenly water" for tea, but teahouses still flourish, some echoing the long traditions of tea drinking in China. In the city's commercial heart you delight in the discovery of a teahouse boasting wood panelling and palms, brass spittoons and gleaming, well-worn teapots, where dignified old men with gold-toothed smiles, gossip and smoke in the company of their songbirds.

Taking yum cha *at a teahouse means doing a bit of business, gossiping and enjoying a variety of* dim sum – *savoury delicacies such as transparent pouches of dough filled with minced shrimp.* Dim sum *literally means "touching the heart" and this they clearly do for the bamboo baskets in which they are served are replenished at a rapid rate.*

mighty clipper ships raced before the northeast monsoons in a bid to win the best prices in London.

It was soon clear that the benison of tea was a mixed blessing, for it threatened to deplete Britain's coffers of silver — until the taipans of the tea trade began smuggling opium into China. The potent sap of the poppy from British India balanced the China trade; fed the opium dreams of China's addicts; and ensured that both tea and opium dominated the early years of the newly acquired colony of Hong Kong.

Whereas tea drinking in Belgrave Square was accompanied by polite conversation over trays laden with silver, at precisely the same hour every day, in China the view was that almost any time was tea time.

Teahouses in China ranged from the simple to the luxurious, the latter luring customers with singsong girls, storytelling, music, miniature gardens and fine porcelain. While such refinements added to the ambience of a teahouse at the top end of the scale, a noisy congestion characterized more basic establishments.

Taking *yum cha* at a teahouse generally meant doing a bit of business, gossiping and enjoying the *dim sum* — savoury delicacies such as transparent pouches of dough filled with minced shrimp — that appeared on every table. The *dim sum* nestled in small round bamboo baskets that could be stacked one on top of another for steaming. The Chinese character for *dim sum* literally meant "touching the heart" and this they clearly did, for the bamboo baskets were emptied and replaced by waitresses at a rapid rate!

Some teahouses catered specifically for bird-lovers who gathered to show off a new cage or the songbird within it. Bird-walking was an ancient custom and the teahouse

Dim sum, *the savoury delicacies served in teahouses, nestle in small round bamboo baskets that are stacked one on top of the other for steaming. Synthetic containers cannot compete — for the bamboo imparts a flavour of its own to the* dim sum, *enabling a centuries-old craft to survive.*

Keeping songbirds in handcrafted cages – furnished perhaps with porcelain bowls or fine carvings of ivory or jade – is an ancient custom still pursued. Supplies of fresh grasshoppers – in their own miniature cages – can be purchased on Bird Street, along with the bamboo, wood or ivory cages that become talking points when bird-fanciers gather.

became an obvious destination — particularly if it attracted bird-fanciers who could debate the merits of mynahs from India, skylarks from Mongolia or flycatchers from Thailand.

Meanwhile the birds vied vocally from a variety of beautifully crafted cages suspended above their owners. Their trilling and carolling added a sweet cadence to the shrilling of waitresses and the clattering of dishes.

Sometimes in the teahouse there was mahjong — the slap of ivory or bamboo tiles added yet another dimension of noise — but always there was talk and tea. Unlike tea drinkers in Europe who favoured black fermented teas, the Chinese preferred fragrant green teas, or the partly fermented oolong teas. Gunpowder was a particular favourite, its smoky flavour heightened by the fresh tang of mint leaves; pale gold jasmine was another, sweetened by the scent of petals of buds. And the names of the different varieties — Cloud Mist, Dragon Well, Po Lei, Lapsang Souchong — were an added source of pleasure.

And when the pot was finished, but the conversation was not, the lid was simply set askew and a replacement appeared made, whenever possible, from the "heavenly water" gathered in huge jars set beneath the teahouse eaves.

In China taking tea in a teahouse had, since ancient time, added pleasure to the pattern of daily life.

In Britain, in the 19th century, the ritual of taking tea became, in itself, infused with the romance of the China trade. For the simple cup of China tea summoned images of ancient walled cities girdled by tea gardens, of mist-enshrouded mountains, and of an emperor with lacquered hair and silken robes who appeared every bit as arrogant as Queen Victoria herself.

These were the images that brought about the China trade, the birth of Hong Kong, and the confrontation of those two mythical creatures: the British Lion and the Chinese Dragon......

A
PHILOSOPHY
OF COSMIC
BALANCE

he Dragon was China's most potent symbol. He lived in the East, source of the winds that carried fertile dust to enrich the fields. His season was spring, when his warm breath quickened new growth in the sere winter earth. His voice was terrible, reverberating in thunder, but it carried with it the blessing of rain. He dwelt in cavernous mountains or the fathomless depths of the ocean, but rose to ride the billowing rain clouds, his talons lancing the earth with the lightning of summer storms. His serpentine neck, bulging eyes and writhing opalescent scales created an awesome spectacle — and the people were ever mindful of his presence, in the air or beneath the earth. So they built their white-washed houses low, so as not to impede his flight, and on sites that would not adversely affect the *Ch'i* or spiritual breath of the universe. For the Dragon — its force positive and creative and male —

embodied the element of Yang, one of two basic components of the Chinese cosmos.

The Dragon was also the spirit of the ancient land.

In China, the ebb and flow of a man's fortune simply reflected the eternal shift of unseen forces — conflicting in times of crises, then coalescing into transitory harmony.

The elements that were the pulse of the cosmos — Yang and Yin, sun and moon, light and dark, heaven and earth, male and female — sought a union that expressed their essential differences while accommodating them within the embrace of a single entity. The Taoist symbol circle.

In the long memory of the land and its people there were countless tales of the consequences of disharmony: of monsoon-swollen rivers swallowing entire villages; of endless droughts when river beds dried and people went hungry. But there was always the patient conviction that harmony

Special blends of herbs, and precious pain-killing balms — distilled from the musk of deers and the gall bladders of bears — fill the brass canisters that gleam in the cool interior of the bonesetter's establishment. Faded ancient tracts are still relevant in a declining profession where skills are handed down from master to apprentice, father to son.

would be restored. Such harmony, in nature and in man, was born of a balance that acknowledged the interdependence of Yin and Yang.

The Chinese believed there was much a man could do to enhance the balance of forces and to shape a fortune that was moulded, by a myriad of unseen powers.

Ancestors, temple gods, earth gods — plus the animistic spirits that inhabited an ancient banyan tree or an outcrop of rock pasted over with crimson-papered prayers — all had the power to influence a man's destiny.

The temple god, gaudy and terrible on an altar laden with offerings, might listen to the heart that was unburdened beneath his gaze. His appearance might be formidable, but he had an acknowledged weakness for sweet incense and the incessant attention of those who sought his help.

He might ease the poverty of a coolie whose rice bowl was seldom full and whose body was wasted by the solace of opium — a coolie who would surely have died unnoticed but for the pity of the gods.

Or he might increase the wealth of a shopkeeper who had never failed to please him and whose fortune he had guided from a humble street stall (where a tiny shrine was never without incense) to an open-fronted shop on a busy street where the altar and its ever present offerings were bathed in the red glow of prosperity.

Within the temples, Buddhist deities often shared a shrine with a Taoist counterpart, for these two religions — plus Confucianism — provided the core of an eclectic mix of beliefs.

Confucian philosophy formed the solid ethical base of a well-ordered society that respected both elders and

The bonesetter's rooms in Shanghai Street afford a glimpse into a fast-disappearing world of healing, eclipsed by the X-ray and modern medicine. Beyond its shuttered doors, carved blackwood chairs line the wall beneath the fading testimonials of customers. In the dim, tranquil interior, the bonesetter awaits customers that do not come — beneath the watchful gaze of an old man in a sepia photograph who established a family tradition.

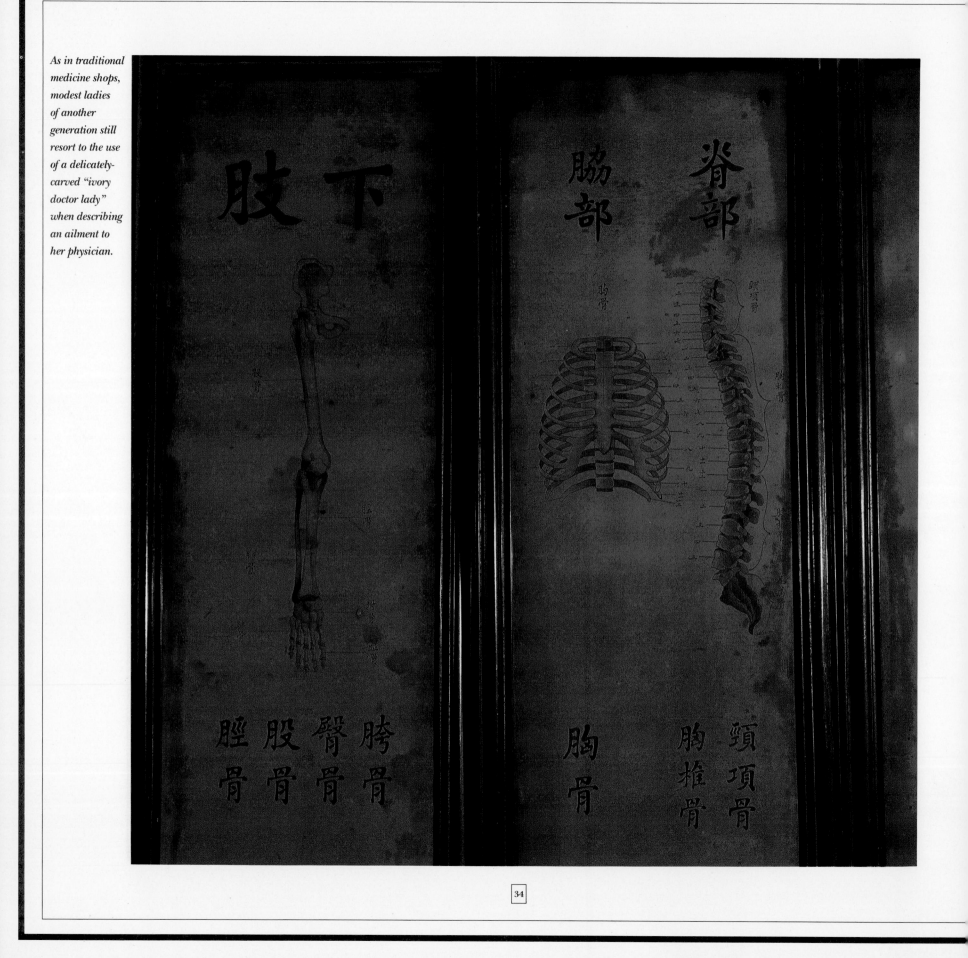

As in traditional medicine shops, modest ladies of another generation still resort to the use of a delicately-carved "ivory doctor lady" when describing an ailment to her physician.

ancestors. Buddhism, imported from India, added notions of reincarnation and purgatory, modified by the innate impulse to better one's lot — in life and death. So departed spirits were offered holidays from hell and in the temple forecourt paper replicas of home comforts — from cars to consorts — were burnt to make life in the underworld more tolerable. Finally, Taoist magic — from exorcism to the manipulation of malevolent spirits — added its own dimension to a blend of beliefs which perfectly reflected the expectations of its creators.

When China was devastated by floods or famine, the people knew that the fine balance of Yin and Yang forces had been disturbed. And when the miniature cosmos of the body suffered a similar imbalance — "too much fire", the physician would say, or "too much water" — a man inevitably succumbed to ailments ranging from the rheumatic aches of "wind in the bones" or a disappointing decline in masculine vigour.

Traditional Chinese medicine was governed by the philosophy of cosmic balance already widely embraced. The body was divided into Yin and Yang organs, each affiliated to one of the Five Elements (wood, earth, fire, metal and water) that also played a vital role in shaping a man's fortune. The heart was a Yin organ generating energy and was thus affiliated to fire; the stomach, a Yang organ, nurtured the body and was therefore related to earth.

The physician based his diagnosis on interpreting the pulse rate and observing the facial features of his patient. His aim was to restore the body's balance by prescribing a blend of ingredients that might include herbs, bark, roots, seeds, fossils, bones, minerals, animal organs, lichens, seaweed, sea horses, insects, antlers and even bat's dung.

When the miniature cosmos of the body suffers an imbalance of its finely-tuned forces — "too much fire", a physician might say, or "too much water" — the body succumbs to ailments that may respond to a beneficial brew of snake blood or bile. In the snake shops of busy Shanghai Street cobras, vipers and other deadly reptiles coil in the darkness of close-packed wooden drawers that line the walls — until an expert handler selects one, deftly removes its gall bladder and prepares a therapeutic brew of green bile with clear rice wine.

The ingredients (each with its own elements of Yin and Yang) were carefully weighed and wrapped in leaves, or folded packages, with instructions regarding their preparations. Others were prepared in the traditional medicine shop, in which case the patient consumed his therapeutic brew on the spot.

In some cases the prescribed medicine came from a nearby snake shop, for both the blood and bile of snakes were considered beneficial. Cobras, vipers and other deadly reptiles writhed in close-packed wooden drawers until an experienced handler removed one and relieved it of its gall bladder — which was conveniently replaced for further prescriptions.

While the curative properties of many Chinese medicines were widely recognized, some seemed to be selected more for their sexual symbolism. Fathering a large family to build the latticework of family ties that spelt security obviously severely taxed the male libido. Confronted by a wife and a string of expectant concubines some sought refuge in the extraordinary selection of materia medica prominently displayed in the traditional medicine shops. The antlers of deer, reputed to be the only animal to have located a sacred fungus bestowing immortality, were cut, dried and sliced or boiled to distil the essence. And if the antlers failed there were alternative remedies from the stag's phallus to dried caterpillars, or the fiery tonic prepared from wild ginseng. While the wealthy could afford the wild ginseng root from the forests of Manchuria and Korea, the man in the street contented himself with the cultivated variety.

With over 10,000 different herbs and substances in the traditional pharmacopoeia, medicine shops — like Chinese temples — offered infinite hope for those in need.

In China, a man of wealth would once have acquired a coffin decades before his death – choosing the finest camphor, regularly lacquered to achieve an awesome sheen. Hong Kong's coffin-makers now work mainly with imported Chinese pine, dyed yellow and waxed to an enhancing golden hue.

A Man's Fortune

nce health was restored the patient would give thanks both to the physician and the deities at the local temple who had a hand in restoring the balance of the body. In fact the business of acknowledging the influence of the gods was so much a part of daily life that the temple itself held none of the awesome formality of a church.

A woman might call at the temple to burn joss sticks at the shrine of a favourite god while on her way to market, having first tended the shrines of earth gods on the outskirts of her village. In the temple square old men read papers, gossiped or played dice in the sunshine. On temple steps worn smooth by the passage of naked feet, women and cripples begged — for those who came to request favours of the gods would wish to appear virtuous.

A porcelain dragon pursuing the pearl of wisdom that all men seek might ornament the ridge of the temple's tiled rooftop, and in the cool of its interior, the slow coil of incense scented the air. Brass urns gleamed, walls were blackened by the smoke of countless offerings, a gong sounded and the candles' glow lit the sheen of a deity's embroidered gown.

In the dim tranquillity, the village or town receded and the dominant sound became the gentle rhythmic shaking of the *chim* by the kneeling worshippers. As bamboo slivers slipped to the floor, messages from the gods were revealed.

A great deal of fortune-telling went on in the temple for the fortune-teller could interpret the unseen forces that were constantly at play in a man's life. He did this in a variety of ways: by interpreting the *chim* sticks in relation to the prayer offered; by consulting the almanac that dictated the tasks that should or should not be undertaken in any

When a man dies, his surviving relatives ensure that his spirit will travel to the afterworld with all the comforts – from paper limousines to comely consorts – that the local paper shop can supply. Fortune-tellers will select a date for the funeral; fung shui men, a suitable location for burial.

Elaborately handcrafted paper creations turn paper shops and temple forecourts into colourful reminders that life is merely an audition for death. In the side streets of Hung Hom and Mongkok, paper shops still produce fantasy mansions, luxury cars, bridges to heaven and money — all that a man will need to ease his life in the afterworld. All are eventually consigned to flames that will destroy their flimsy earthly form and carry them to the awaiting spirits.

Temple gods have an acknowledged weakness for sweet incense, and the incessant attention of those who seek their help. Turning ground sandalwood into joss sticks is Hong Kong's oldest industry, and the incense once shipped to Canton may well have given the island its name – Fragrant Harbour.

one day; and by reading palms and facial features. Moles and blemishes were all significant in physiognomy and much faith was placed in this form of fortune-telling. In fact, in Imperial China the right kind of face could qualify a candidate for official appointment.

Fortune-tellers were consulted before any important decisions were taken, particularly if they related to birth, marriage and death.

When a man died his spirit took a triple form: one accompanied the body to the grave in a coffin carved from Chinese pine; another travelled to the underworld with all the comforts the local paper shop could provide; while a third resided in the ancestral tablets in the home or local temple. All three spirits had to be tended lest they became the restless "hungry ghosts" that wandered the world inflicting hardship on the living.

The fortune-teller would set an auspicious date for the funeral, and a *fung shui* ("wind and water" man) would advise a burial site that would not disturb the essential harmony of mountains, winds, water and dragon spirits.

A man's fortune was calculated in relation to the hour, day, month and year of his birth. Each year in the cycle of 60 was denoted by a combination of one of the all-important five elements and 12 animals of the zodiac.

When a marriage was to be arranged, no formal steps were taken until the local fortune-teller had pronounced the couple's horoscopes to be harmonious. If they were not, the fortune-teller might advise his client to seek a more compatible candidate.

"This is a fire girl", he might advise an anxious mother. "She will consume a wood husband such as your son. Go and look for a water girl who will nourish him..."

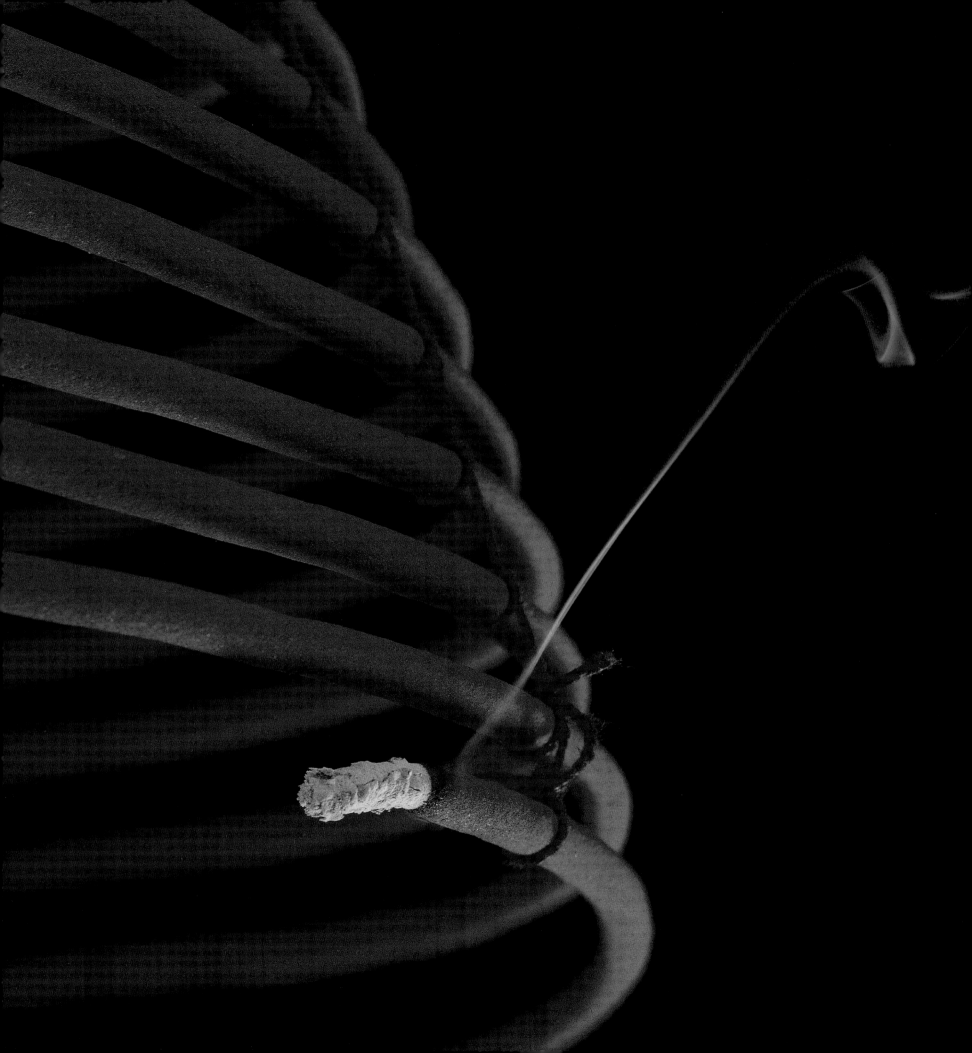

In the dim tranquillity of the local temple the
slow coil of incense scents the air. The clamour
of the restless city recedes and the dominant
sound becomes the gentle rhythmic shaking of
the chim by kneeling worshippers. As a single
bamboo sliver slips to the floor, messages from
the gods are revealed. . . . . .

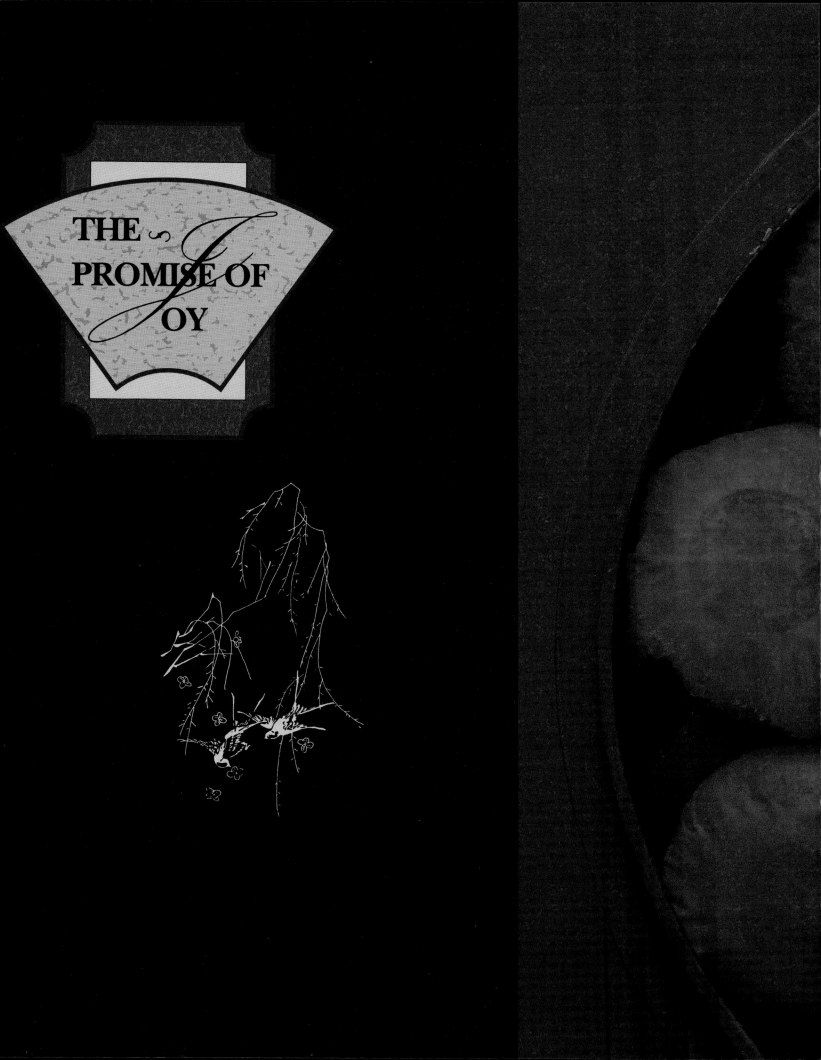

THE PROMISE OF JOY

In China, when a girl married, her long black hair — once braided — would be swept up in a knot stiffened with resin and held by gold pins. Her rouged face was a mask beneath the tasselled, pearl-encrusted phoenix coronet.

Weeks of seclusion and lamenting — for the loss of family and a familiar town or village — ended on the morning of her wedding day.

She bathed in an infusion of pummelo leaves that would wash away all traces of ill-fortune. Attended by a "good luck woman" chosen for her long and happy marriage and her capacity to produce children, she donned her wedding gown.

Later, when she left her home, she was carried across the threshold — and a pan of glowing charcoal — to ensure she took away none of her family's good fortune.

It must have seemed to the bride, that day, that everything around her was washed in the auspicious red that promised joy and good fortune. Her embroidered wedding *kwa* and silk shoes were red, and she was carried to her new home in a red bridal sedan embellished with gilt and flowers.

As the picture-book procession moved through fields of gold (for harvest was considered a good time for rural weddings), it was headed by wedding lanterns bearing the names of the betrothed. Music, gongs, drums and the chatter of firecrackers marked the route that had been planned to avoid contact with bad omens ranging from wells to widows. Meanwhile, lurking spirits were distracted with scattered rice or a succulent baked pig borne before the bridal sedan.

Bearers surrounding the bridal chair carried a dowry that

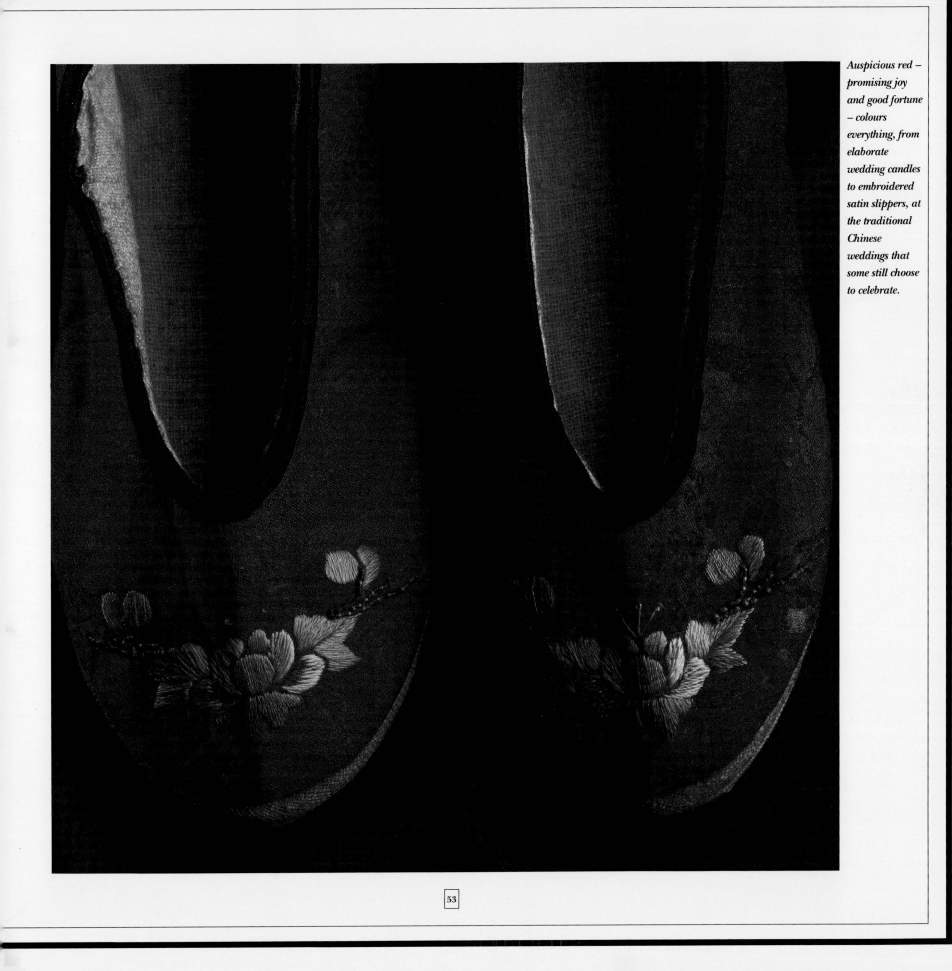

Auspicious red – promising joy and good fortune – colours everything, from elaborate wedding candles to embroidered satin slippers, at the traditional Chinese weddings that some still choose to celebrate.

was the subject of much gossip and scrutiny — fine redwood furniture inlaid with marble perhaps, or camphorwood chests of porcelain and jade. The groom's family would also have broadcast the generosity of their gifts to the bride's family. Once the birth dates had been matched for harmony, gifts were presented as an acknowledgment of the betrothal.

On arrival at the groom's house the couple would pay their respects to the ancestors whose blessing had already been sought. Prior to the betrothal the birth dates of the couple had been placed beneath the ancestral tablets. The groom's family had then watched for bad omens — the death of stock, or family feuds — that might indicate ancestral anxiety over the proposed union.

The bride and groom would then share a cup of wine and honey, and later the bride would serve tea to a bevy of mothers-in-law intent on extracting revenge for the remembered humiliations they suffered as young brides or concubines.

The young girl decked in red would have had few illusions about the life that lay before her. Owing unquestioned obedience to both her husband and mothers-in-law, she could be divorced for reasons ranging from infertility to verbosity.

Having submitted to the father who arranged her marriage to his advantage, she would now submit to the man who lifted her red veil and saw her face — probably for the first time.

THE $\mathscr{S}$TONE OF IMMORTALITY

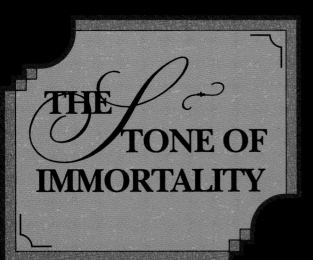

The Chinese bride would value jade above gold as a wedding gift. A pair of carved butterflies for double happiness. A jade ornament for the hair. Or a pendant carved to the contours of a fish — for the fish, being fecund and happy in its element was a symbol of happy marriage.

Legend has it that even in the earth gold and jade were antagonistic for while the appeal of gold was material, that of jade was spiritual.

Certainly no other stone in history could claim such a close affinity or such a significant spiritual role in the life of a nation. For the limpid stone, believed to link heaven and earth, belonged to the realm of legend.

The Chinese believe its origins go back to the dawn of creation when the god Pan Ku carved the universe and, at death, became part of his creations. His head became mountains, his breath the wind and clouds, his flesh and blood the soil and rivers, and the marrow of his bones became jade.

Over the years the stone's mystique became as potent as its beauty. An emperor of China is said to have offered 15 cities for a jade carving he could hold in the palm of his hand. And when China was invaded by the Tartars, who subjugated the people of Han, the Imperial Dragon wept tears that petrified to jade within the earth.

Because it had the power to bridge heaven and earth, life and immortality, the emperor, praying on behalf of the Children of Han, used a circular *pi* disc (carved in jade and representing heaven) to transmit his appeal to the gods. Ancestral tablets which linked the living with the dead, were also carved in jade and when men of substance died, jade was placed in their tombs to preserve their bodies.

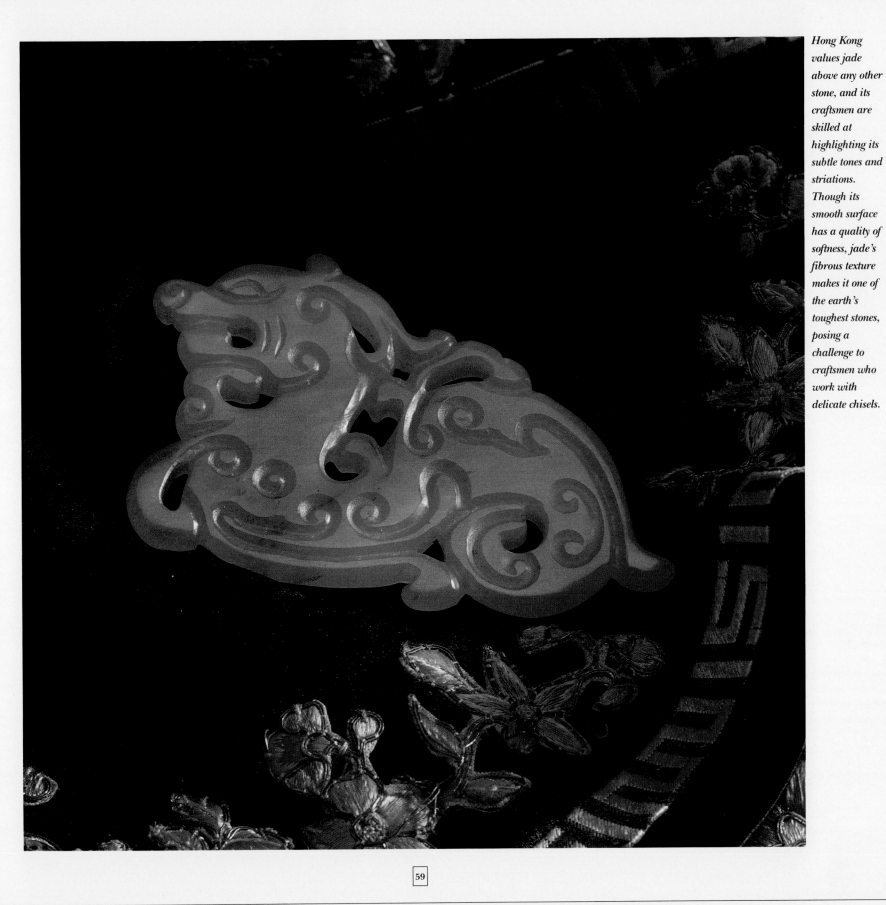

Hong Kong values jade above any other stone, and its craftsmen are skilled at highlighting its subtle tones and striations. Though its smooth surface has a quality of softness, jade's fibrous texture makes it one of the earth's toughest stones, posing a challenge to craftsmen who work with delicate chisels.

The tombs of old emperors thus became a magnet for grave robbers whose exploits accounted for much of the old jade in circulation today. Those who violated the tombs of the noble or wealthy risked certain death, but were handsomely rewarded for their precious plunder. Tombs were often cleverly concealed and at least one contained crossbows set to shoot automatically. This tomb contained not only the body of the emperor, but those of his concubines — and the artisans unlucky enough to know the secrets of the tomb.

Admired for its glowing beauty and enduring strength, jade was a talisman prized by all. Even the poorest peasant woman cherished her lucky "chicken heart" finger jade that ensured fertility, and her children wore jade bangles, pendants and charms to ward off disease or the jealousy of disaffected spirits.

Chinese craftsmen had worked with jade since ancient times and had perfected the art of revealing its subtle tones and striations. Though its cool, smooth surface had a quality of softness, jade's fibrous texture made it one of the earth's toughest stones. As such it posed a challenge to craftsmen creating a carving that would best express the inherent qualities of the stone and the endless hues of its spectrum. Jade ranged from pink to purple, from gold to green and even the latter boasted over a hundred different shades from "spring water green" to "moss entangled in the snow".

Marco Polo had admired the beauty of the stone carved with such skill by craftsmen in the court of Kublai Khan. However, as with the secret of silk, China guarded its jade and forbade its export. Jade was mined in only a few precious pockets scattered across the world and there is no evidence to suggest it was ever mined on a significant scale in China. The nephrite for carvings came from Turkestan while Burma was the source of the emerald jewel jade, or jadeite, that women found so enhancing against the skin.

The Chinese believed that the polish of the stone they revered represented purity; its dense toughness suggested resolution and intelligence; its clean angles brought to mind justice; while its transparency symbolized sincerity.

And in the hands of the most gifted craftsmen, the stone of immortality seemed to possess a life of its own — an inner glow that merely added to its mystique.

60

REVERENCE FOR THE WRITTEN WORD

When the first emperor of a unified China ordered his craftsman to carve an imperial seal, he naturally selected jade as the material. The Seal of Succession became an enduring symbol of the right to rule — the Mandate of Heaven — and it was decreed that no one but the emperor could use a seal of jade.

Seals were the most ancient identification, and reverence for the written character coupled with the skill of engravers ensured that they also became miniature works of art.

The illiterate peasant would use a wooden seal to identify himself in correspondence prepared for him by the local letter writer. A scholar might devote hours selecting the material for his personal seal which could be embellished with a miniature bas-relief landscape or mounted by an auspicious symbol. Mandarins and military officials would issue edicts stamped with their seals — for every official had a seal of office that was closely guarded.

Seal engravers combined the skills of calligraphist with those of master carver, but the design he created had to be carved within a square, circle or rectangle that might measure less than two centimetres.

Painters and calligraphists were often also skilled engravers, for no painting was complete without its inscription and seal. Sometimes a well-respected connoisseur would add his own personal seal of approval beside an artist's who had created a fine painting or scroll of calligraphy.

The preparation and quality of the vermilion used by the engraver was considered vital in the appreciation of seals. Made from pulverized cinnabar and oil, soaked on a stamp pad made from the fibres of the moxa plant, the ingredients were occasionally fanciful. The Emperor Ch'ien-lung's vermilion was made from pearl, coral, ruby and cinnabar — and his seals have not faded over 300 years.

Some of the oldest seals in China were made from bronze, but the invention of paper in the second century popularized engraving and introduced a range of materials including gold, silver, horn, crystal, ivory, clay, porcelain, amber and stone from China's most famous quarries.

Characters of Captivating Beauty Along with paper and printing China also introduced to the world the first civil service staffed by scholar officials. Anyone could sit the examinations for official appointments, but to succeed a scholar had to write elegant prose and poetry (which echoed the classics), be well-versed in literature, and produce fine calligraphy.

Every scholar tried to excel in painting, seal engraving and calligraphy — for the three were viewed as inseparable — but calligraphy was considered the highest art form.

The Chinese never looked upon their writing merely as the medium of communication. The ancient pictograph formed the basis for an abiding affinity between painting and writing and turned a utilitarian sign into a character of captivating beauty.

As the slow process of shaping the script took hold of the Chinese imagination, it brought with it the recognition that calligraphy could be an art in its own right. The literati were soon experimenting with their own stylistic embellishments to the script, but when the first Ch'in dynasty emperor

assumed power in a unified China, he swept aside such sophistication, ordering that the written language be simplified and standardized.

Boldness, Energy or Lyricism The invention of paper and bristle brushes (replacing shaved wood or bamboo and reed pen or bronze stylus) released calligraphy from early restraints. Now it truly flowered into an art that invited practitioners to invest each stroke, line, dash or hook with the boldness, energy or lyricism they wished to express.

Over the centuries Chinese characters have been shaped by a long process of stylization and abstraction. A character could stand alone, representing a simple object, or be a compound of several characters expressing an abstract idea.

When a calligraphist set to work on a scroll he could envisage the brush strokes that would break the white expanse: the powerful down strokes, the sensuous curves, the bold dashes and the delicate lines — fine as silk — that would link one movement with the next.

When he lifted his brush his arm seemed to be drawn by the lines of the characters he expressed.

Painting, seal engraving and calligraphy are viewed as inseparable arts, and painters and calligraphists are often also skilled engravers – for no painting is complete without its inscription and the vermilion seal of its creator.

Surrounded by the tools of his trade — the brushes that describe both the bold down strokes and the silk-fine lines that invest calligraphy with its captivating beauty — the calligraphist is a symbol of the artistry of another era that lingers in the 20th century. For the Chinese never looked upon writing merely as a means of communication — reverence for the written word turned calligraphy into visual poetry.

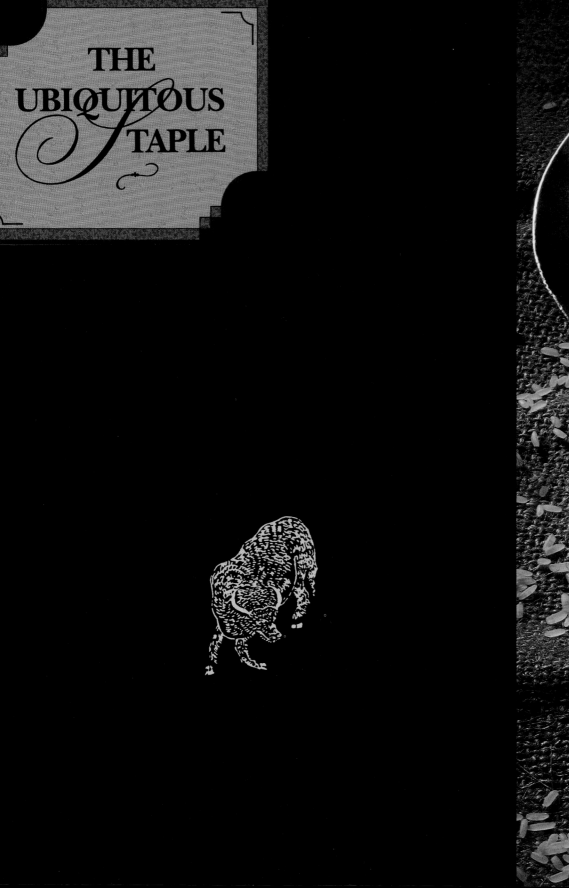

THE
UBIQUITOUS
STAPLE

The early pictograph not only communicated an image or idea, it reflected the life of the nation itself. The character for field became four plots surrounded by irrigation trenches, while that of a well — eight plots centred around a communal well — told of the sense of communal cooperation that was the strength of a nation bound to the land.

Over the centuries China's landscape was contoured, patterned and coloured by a single staple which, more than any other, nourished the hungry nation. And the rice that shaped the landscape also shaped the character of the people. For the Chinese had always lived with the spectre of famine, so they put every acre of arable land to use and coaxed the earth to yield harvests that fed more people than anywhere else in the world. Together they maintained the mud dykes that sculptured the landscape. And

together they planted the seedlings, flooded the fields, transplanted and harvested the rice that later dried in the sun on rooftops.

The stored rice promised security for the circle of faces — bowls raised and chopsticks clicking — that gathered to share the morning and evening rice. And when the harvest lay gold against the backdrop of blue mountains, the people thanked the gods who had guarded their fields with vigilance and averted the droughts or floods that left their rice bowls empty.

The cultivation of rice thus became interwoven with the social, moral and religious life of the nation. There was a time when the emperor himself planted the first rice of the season and at harvest time each village sent an annual tribute of rice to the Son of Heaven.

Several thousand varieties of rice were cultivated south of

Over the centuries China's landscape was contoured and patterned by a single staple that both nourished the nation and shaped the character of its people. Stored rice promised security for villagers who gathered to savour the leisure of evening after a day of toil in the paddy fields.

73

the mighty Yangtze River in provinces blessed with ample sunshine and luxuriant rain.

It seemed, in these provinces, that village life had always gravitated around the local paddy fields, for rice had been the staple since the 4th century. It both sustained and shaped Chinese society, making incredible demands on those whose life depended on the endless cycle of its cultivation.

The transplanting of seedlings from nursery beds to paddies would involve entire families in dawn to dusk toil, for the orderly lines of young plants had to be pressed into the soft mud before the sun's heat grew too intense.

When the fields were drained and ready to yield their gold, every man, woman and child was needed to help with harvesting, threshing, marketing and storing the crop. Dried stalks were gathered for cooking fuel or winter

warmth before the land was cleared and ploughed for a winter crop of beans or, where winters were benign, a second or third rice crop.

But before the fields could be flooded and ploughed by water buffaloes, the contoured rice terraces, the irrigation canals and the dykes all required inspection and repairs.

The relentless demands of the rice cycle moulded strong family networks and close cooperative communities well aware that their survival depended on good husbandry and a unified effort to thwart the storms, floods and droughts summoned up by vengeful gods.

However, when drought, floods or civil strife that disrupted the rice cycle consistently emptied the nation's rice bowl, the people suspected that a higher force was at work: that the Mandate of Heaven was being withdrawn from the emperor.

In the noodle factory, machines and men are covered with fine white flour they work with in producing the rice noodles that have long been favoured in Hong Kong. The rice dough can also be expertly pulled and folded by hand, producing a skein of fine noodles that will be sold fresh or dried, in markets and noodle shops.

It was considered that the emperor's highest duty was to see his people fed — and indeed imperial revenues were dependant on the gold of bountiful harvests. So when, in the 10th century, the rice crop failed, the emperor ordered the distribution of early ripening champa rice, imported from Vietnam. This variety of rice, along with a system of canals that tamed the vagaries of rivers that either flooded or dwindled, transformed vast hitherto unproductive areas of the south. Soon, in terms of population and riches, the south was rivalling the longer-established north. The abundance of southern harvests spawned a network of roads and canals which, along with broad rivers, carried rice to the imperial court and to the emperor's vast armies, stationed in the north to deter barbarian invaders.

Ever mindful of the trinity of forces — Heaven, Earth and Man — that worked together to extract the richest possible harvest, the emperor conducted two awesome ceremonies each year. The Sacrifice to Heaven was performed at the winter solstice and was rich in symbolic rites. A silent pre-dawn procession, screened by lengths of blue-green cloth, moved from the Forbidden City to the Temple of Heaven where silk and jade were offered to heaven from a circular (Yang) alter facing north. During the summer solstice, the gods were offered yellow jade and silk from a square (Yin) alter facing south.

In the early 1830s when the nation was plagued with floods, famine and insurrections — plus the unwanted intrusions of opium-smuggling barbarians — the Son of Heaven made a heartfelt plea to ease China's torment. On the night of the winter solstice the emperor, wearing an antique robe embroidered with sacred symbols — the

Open-air markets flower wherever the city can accommodate them — in spacious squares that become arenas of riotous colour and sound; or in narrow alleys filled with the mingled flavours of street-side kitchens, garlic and tobacco. Here you will find "100-year-old eggs" displayed in the fine ornamental jars in which they are preserved, stored and transported.

Coated with a mixture of lime, salt and ash, "100-year-old eggs"— that have probably been preserved for a hundred days – are shelled and sliced when ready to eat. Their distinctive patterned shells are familiar in stalls which may also sell quail, pigeon and salted eggs preserved in brine.

dragon, sun, moon and rice — appealed to Heaven on behalf of the drought-striken earth.

His plea, accompanied by sacrifices of buffalo, incense, jade and silk, and oblations of wine — did not go unheeded. That very night a great armada of dark clouds massed on the horizon bringing the sustained, heaven-sent rain that would revive the earth — and the rice cycle.

Being frugal and resourceful, the people of China used not only the grains of rice but also its flowers (as a dentifrice), its stalks and ash (medicinal) and its straw (for matting, rope, paper and thatch).

And when it came to cooking the *fan* they were equally inventive. Rice was boiled, baked, steamed, fried, ground and dried. It was turned into dough which, when expertly pulled and folded, produced a skein of fine rice noodles that were sold fresh or dried in markets and noodle shops.

Rice was ubiquitous in China. It dried on straw mats, on rooftops or on the side of the road, was carried on barges that plied the rivers, steamed in bowls at foodstalls, was served as glutinous dumplings at the Feast of the Fifth Moon, and was turned into the fiery wine that accompanied banquets.

Just as village life revolved around the paddy fields that provided yields in excess of any other crop, so meal time centred around the nutritious and tasteful staple. Rice formed the basis of every meal, providing a bed for frugally chopped meat, fish, eggs and vegetables. Food was diced and fast-cooked to save scarce fuel, to yield the maximum flavour and nutrition, and to retain the vivid colours of vegetables. For colour and texture, as well as taste, were deemed as vital to a meal as the balance of hot and cold dishes, sweet and sour flavours, and spicey and bland

Hong Kong's earliest settlers were fisherfolk who chased shoals across the South China Seas. These hardy people dried the best of their catch for times when shoals were less abundant – and the sight of fish drying on rooftops remains common in outlying villages that still depend on the ocean's harvest.

seasonings. In food, as in life, the pervasive Yin/Yang philosophy was at work, and seeking a satisfactory balance was always the guiding principle.

If rice was an integral part of every meal, the open-air market played a similarly vital role in any Chinese city. Here you could buy the rice and every other fresh ingredient that would grace a banquet table, or a simple family meal.

Markets flourished wherever a city could accommodate them — in spacious squares that became arenas of riotous colour and sound; or in narrow alleys filled with the mingled flavours of street-side kitchens, fresh fish, garlic and tobacco.

Stalls were laden with wet fresh fruit and vegetables — emerald and red peppers, plump purple eggplants, golden oranges and pumpkins, melons and courgettes, tomatoes and tropical fruits. Snakes might coil in jars; pigs would protest; shiny, slippery fish would slap the pavement while pigeons and quails demurely await their certain fate.

And if the shopper's taste buds were tantalized by the sight of so much good food, there were dozens of itinerant street-side chefs shouting enticements for sizzling pork, steaming noodles, deep-fried sticky rice balls plus the seasonal delights — like mooncakes in autumn — that abounded in every market. And among the foodstalls were barbers, fortune-tellers, letter writers, chiropodists, porcelain-menders and, in a colourful corner — a lantern-maker working his magic with bright silk and paper, wood and bamboo.

THE
SYMBOL
OF
Light

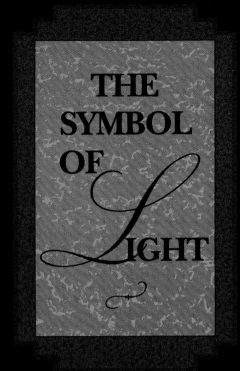

When the rice in the paddies deepened to emerald and then the gold of harvest, farmers never failed to hang lanterns in their fields to frighten off malevolent spirits. For in China the lantern was a symbol of light — of Yang — and no social or religious celebration was complete without displays of auspicious red lanterns.

Sometimes villagers combined the two powerful symbols of light and goodness in the form of a 100-foot-long "dragon lantern". As many as 80-jointed lanterns, suspended from poles, separated snapping jaws and a thrashing tail. As the dragon lantern snaked through the field it carried with it a fearsome cacophony of drums, gongs and exploding firecrackers.

From ancient times a Lantern Festival welcomed the light and warmth of spring, and later, when summer's heat was eclipsed by the cool of autumn an essentially feminine festival ushered in the prettiest of lanterns. During the Moon Festival young girls burnt incense and candles and whispered prayers to the matchmaker on the moon, but for the children the delight of the festival was the lanterns themselves. At Moon Festival time the lantern-maker truly indulged his flights of fancy with symbolic lanterns (butterflies for longevity, lobsters for mirth) in the shapes of birds, insects, fish and animals.

In old Peking there was a famous street of lantern stalls which, on market days, was festive with colour. Rich and poor came to Lantern Market Street, for lanterns had always been considered indispensable in China. The humblest peasant would not venture out at night without one, and mandarins and military officials, travelling across the country in sedan chairs, always displayed their titles on the lanterns that lit their paths.

The eclipse of summer's heat by the cool of autumn has always ushered in the most magical festival of the lunar year. On the night of the Moon Festival, young girls burn incense and whisper prayers to the match-maker on the moon in the glow of fanciful lanterns.

The lantern is a symbol of light – of Yang – and no social or religious celebration is complete without colourful lanterns in symbolic shapes. Lantern-makers, whose families have practised the craft for generations, constantly indulge in new flights of fancy to light the festivals of the lunar year.

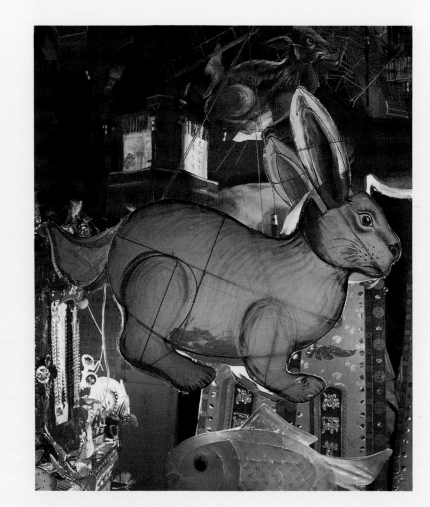

Lantern-makers, whose families had practised the craft for generations, were constantly devising new designs and trying new materials for their handwork. Fancy silken lanterns, tasselled and ornamented with pearls or jade, were fashioned for wealthy mandarins. Silk or paper lanterns, exquisitely painted with scenes from legends, appealed to connoisseurs. However, the simple man contented himself with a basic lantern of bamboo and waxed paper, or a lattice-work lantern fashioned from split bamboo covered with waxed paper coated with glue and varnished to transparency. Lanterns were also made from wood, gauze, glass, transparent horn or even stalks of wheat. There was even one — which military men might favour — on which figures of warriors on horseback (set on a revolving base) endlessly chased one another as the candle's hot air rotated them. But the simplest lanterns were those made by children in autumn when ancestral graves were swept and made ready for winter. Candles were set in the hollow of lotus leaves. They glowed green and gave untold delight — if only for a night.

There was a time when most of the windows of China were made of paper pasted damp over the wooden lattice frames — in much the same way as lanterns. The paper was replaced at Chinese New Year, when small red "window flower" papercuts were pasted on the inside of the new windows.

When dusk fell and lamps were lit, each simple house became a large-scale lantern, each street a place of instant beauty and gaiety.

Or so it must have seemed to lovers and poets......

A
PRICELESS
HERITAGE

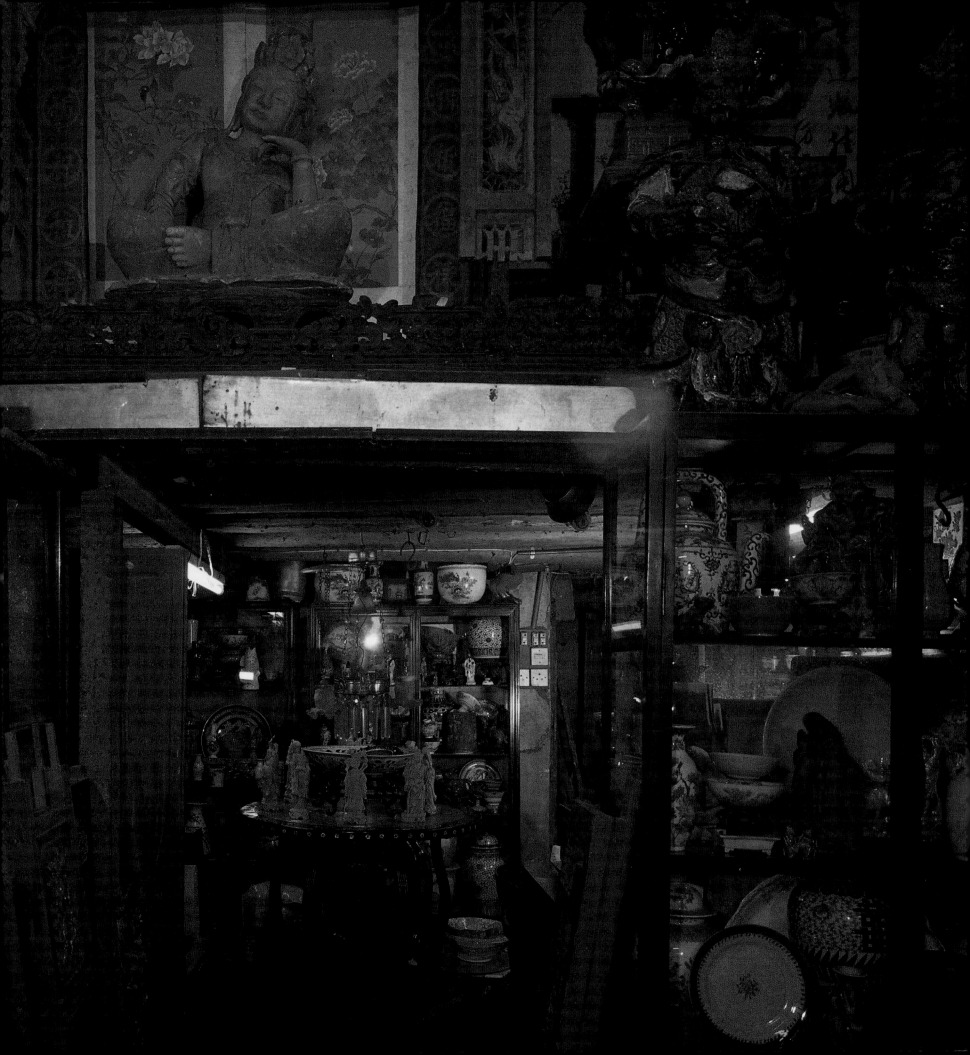

hinese lanterns — so simple, so magic — have cast their glow down thousands of years of Chinese history. And still they light the festivals of Hong Kong today, though no one knows if the lantern-maker will still be creating his fanciful designs into the next century.

For the traditional shops that still add colour and character to Hong Kong's streets, chances of survival seem tenuous. Though temples still lure people of all ages, paper shops are dying with the generation of worshippers who demand them. While traditional medicine shops are busy and have revealed ancient cures for contemporary complaints (sea horses are also efficacious for high cholesterol levels!), the bonesetter concedes he has no young apprentice to whom he can pass the skills he acquired from a master, or the knowledge accrued through years of practice. Certainly teahouses still add a distinctive noisy clamour to the city's street sounds, but the teashop, its

containers filled with aromatic blends, seems certain to be swallowed by supermarkets or upmarket gourmet shops.

Hong Kong has always had an insatiable appetite for the new and innovative. It has made it its business to be in the forefront of both the production and consumption of 20th-century technology. It is addicted to fads and fashions that are rapidly replaced — which is good for business. So in this most aggressive, sales-orientated city, no one is gambling on the future of a handful of shops that are links with an almost fabled past.

What is certain is that if the traditional shops disappear, Hong Kong, in common with other fast-growing Asian cities, will have lost much more than just a little "local colour".

It will have lost an element of heritage that — unlike the merchandise that fills its ever-expanding shop windows — is both priceless and irreplaceable.

The fung shui
compass, the
fan, the lantern,
the abacus
objects the
Chinese have
valued through
the ages – linger
as reminders of
Old China in an
age, and in a
city, that
celebrates the
technology of
today.

A handful of shops, a collection of once-prized objects, and the master craftsman who still labours over things of beauty — all are the last links with Old China. If they disappear Hong Kong will have shed more than a little "local colour". It will have lost an element of heritage that — unlike the merchandise that currently fills its shop windows — is priceless and irreplaceable.

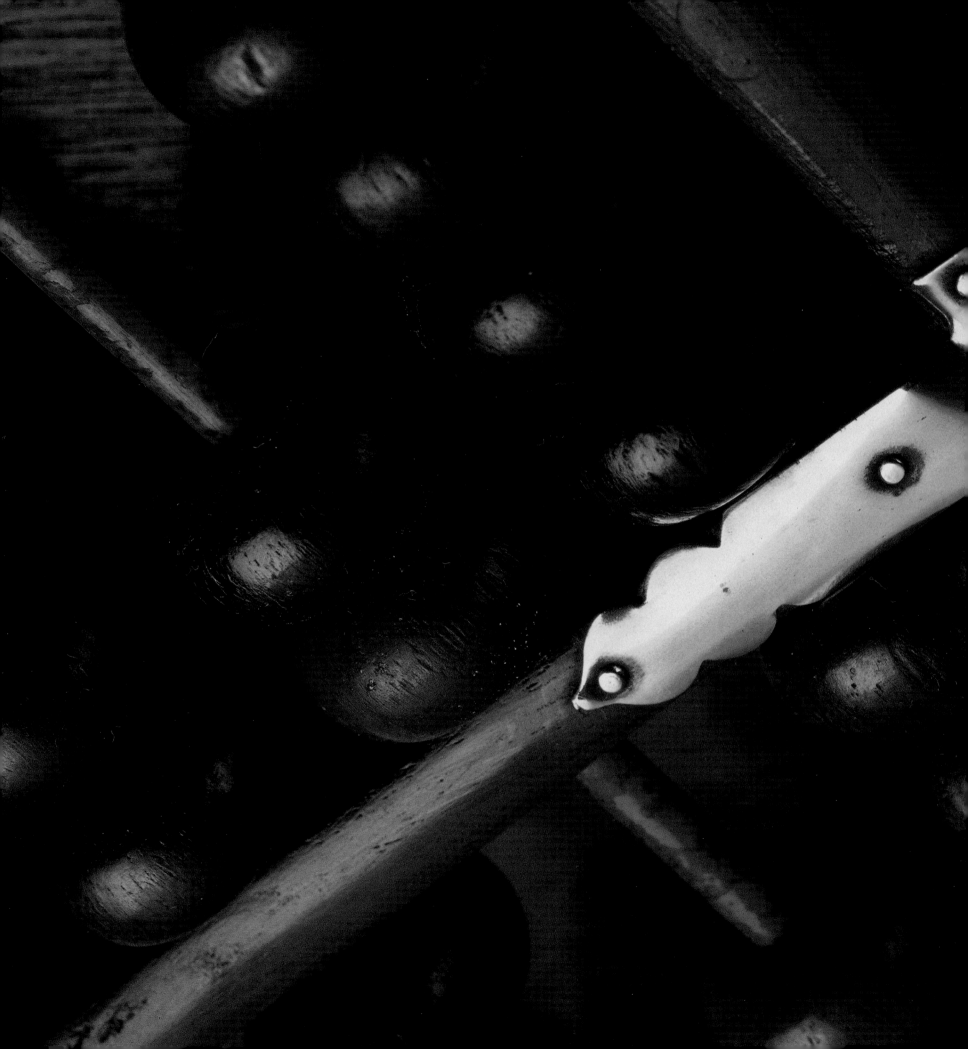